TREASURE HUNT
IN THE
CREEPY MANSION

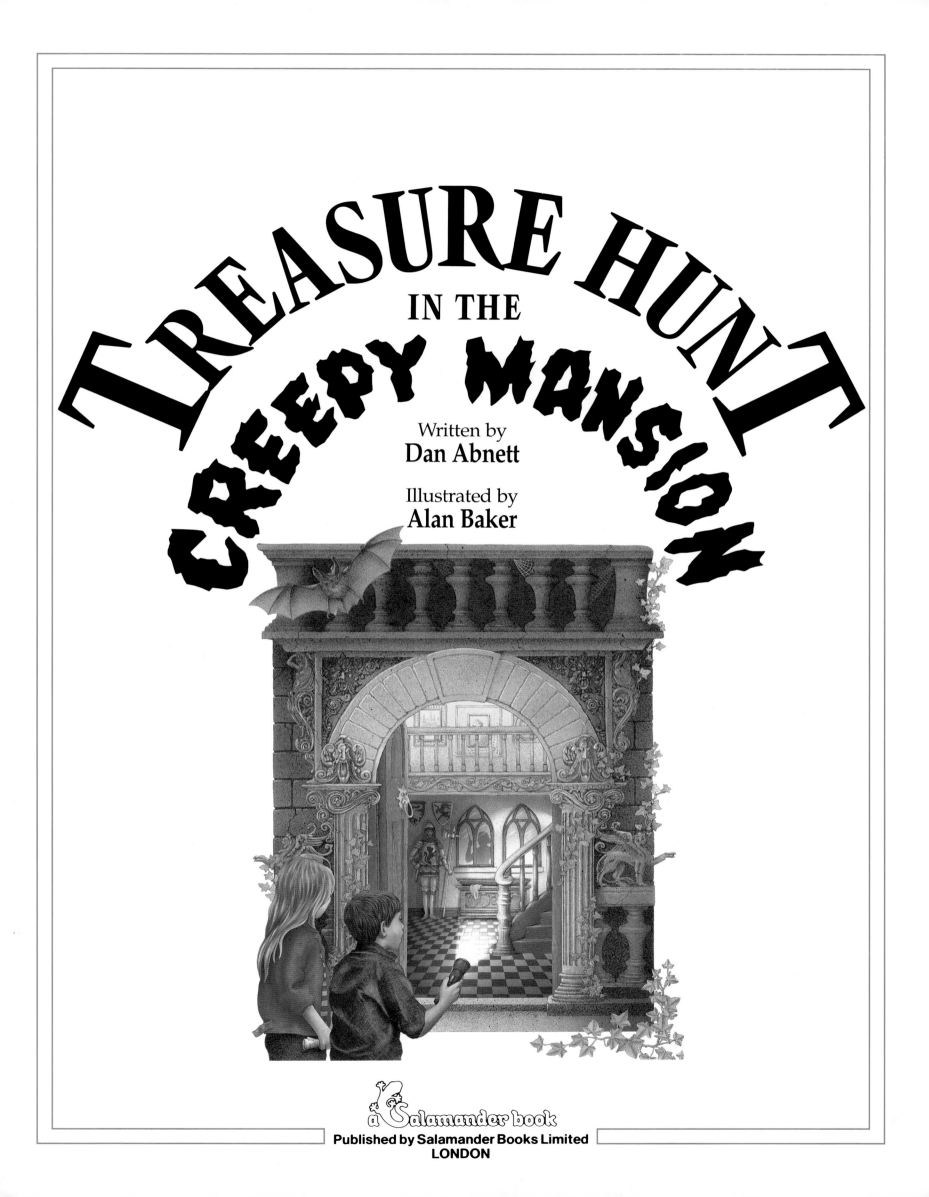

TREASURE HUNT
IN THE
CREEPY MANSION

Written by
Dan Abnett

Illustrated by
Alan Baker

a Salamander book

Published by Salamander Books Limited
LONDON

A SALAMANDER BOOK

Published by Salamander Books Ltd.,
129-137 York Way,
London N7 9LG,
United Kingdom.

© Salamander Books Ltd., 1995

Distributed by Random House Value Publishing, Inc.
40 Engelhard Avenue
Avenel, New Jersey 07001

A CIP catalog record for this book is available from the Library of Congress.

ISBN 0-517-14026-8

1 3 5 7 9 8 6 4 2

CREDITS

Editor: Helen Stone
Designer: Rachael Stone
Color separation by: Pixel Tech, Singapore
Printed in China

YOUR QUEST BEGINS HERE...

Robert and Anna, two intrepid treasure hunters, have gathered together some clues, which they believe point to hidden treasure lurking in the creepy mansion owned by Mister Strange. They are about to set off for the mansion any minute, but if you think you have enough courage and are smart enough for such an adventure, you are invited to join them in their quest

If you choose to accept the challenge, waste no time and make your way immediately to the mansion. Once inside, you should travel from room to room

collecting further clues and solving puzzles and riddles along the way. You will be given a choice of routes to take, so your path through the mansion is entirely up to you. It is an odd building with interconnecting rooms and many secret passages so, from time to time you may find yourself back in a place that you have already passed through. If you have already solved the puzzles and have collected any necessary clues the room has to offer, go straight to the directions, which tell you where to visit next. Keep your wits about you. This challenge will only be solved by the most eagle-eyed and clever sleuth.

Good luck, treasure hunter!

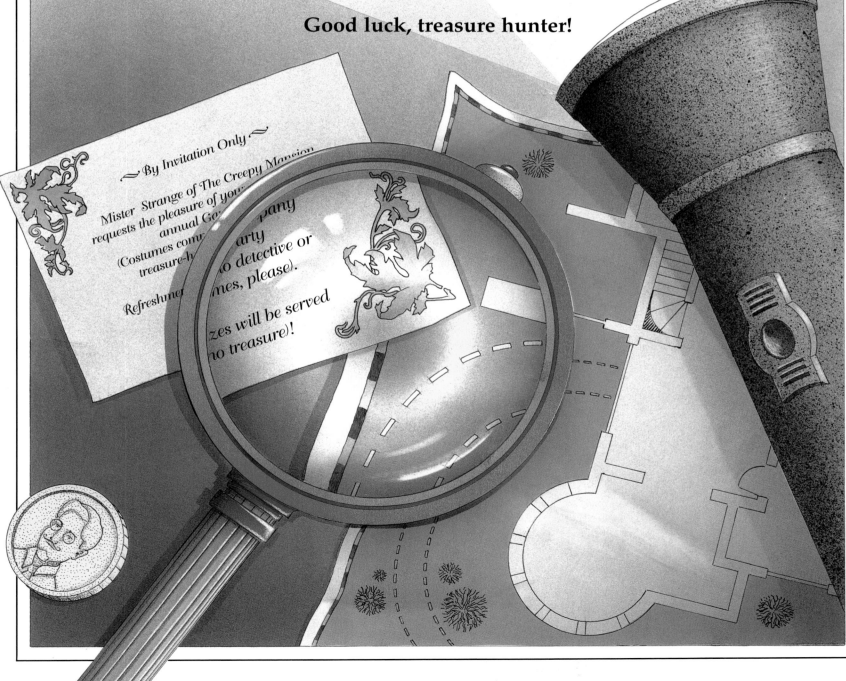

IN

THE MAIN ENTRANCE

"According to the map, this is the place," said Robert, eyeing the huge cast iron gates.

"Well, it sure looks creepy enough to me," replied Anna, "but how do we get inside?"

"I can't see a latch to undo, but if this map is anything to go by, this isn't the only way in."

"I don't mind which way we go. Let's just get inside now. I feel like we're being watched and it's giving me the creeps," said Anna with a shudder.

The old gate is a maze. Follow the maze to the center symbol to release the secret catch. Anna was right about being watched. How many people can you see hiding in the mansion grounds? If you have managed to unlock the gate, turn to page 8. If you prefer to sneak in the back entrance, turn to page 16.

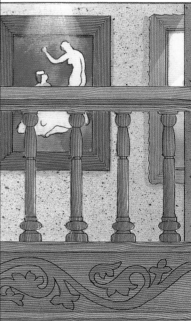

THE MAIN HALL

"Wow, what an amazing place! It looks like someone is clearing things out, but I can't imagine who would want to throw out such beautiful objects!" said Robert.

"No one in their right mind would throw out any of these things, for they are all priceless and irreplaceable, each and every one!" said Graves, the butler, in his most commanding voice. "In fact, that is why they have been boxed up for storage. The Master has many house guests and cannot risk his most prized possessions being damaged. However, I think the maid has been a little over-zealous. I note that the Master's favorite painting, which once took pride of place on the wall to my right, has vanished. As has the replica of the portrait of the late Mister Egnarts, which the Master had commissioned as a gift for Lady Smartly. These things must be found before the Master discovers that they are missing."

"Well, please allow us to help you look!" said Anna.

8

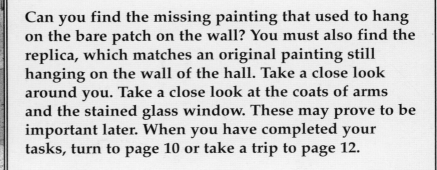

Can you find the missing painting that used to hang on the bare patch on the wall? You must also find the replica, which matches an original painting still hanging on the wall of the hall. Take a close look around you. Take a close look at the coats of arms and the stained glass window. These may prove to be important later. When you have completed your tasks, turn to page 10 or take a trip to page 12.

THE TROPHY PASSAGE

"Wow! Look at all these strange beasts! Are they real?" said Anna in amazement.

"Well, the Master has traveled to some very unusual places," said Graves in a matter-of-fact manner.

"Can we take a closer look?" asked Robert

"You may, indeed. But beware, the floor is very old and unstable. It is prone to shift and crumble without a moment's notice," replied Graves. "You may walk from one end of the corridor to the other in perfect safety as long as you follow just one row of the patterned tiles, and only one row is completely safe."

10

Trace your finger along the rows of tiles leading from one end of the corridor to the other. Add up the number of sides of the patterns in each row of tiles. The row that has 21 patterned tiles with a total of 63 sides is the one to follow. Once you have found the safe path, turn to page 12 or page 16, but before you leave, see how many hidden creatures you can find other than those on display.

THE MASTER'S STUDY

"You are very honored," said Graves cooly. "Very few people have ever had the privilege of being inside Mister Strange's private study."

"Well, he must be a very clever man. Just look at all these books!" said Anna, studying the bookcase.

"Well, he can't be that clever!" retorted Robert. "He hasn't managed to finish this puzzle."

"The Master is a busy man and does not have much time for such trifling exercises," explained Graves, in a weary tone.

Can you find the two pieces that would complete the puzzle? When you have found the solution, continue your quest by turning to page 14 or go to page 18. Before you leave the study, select one item to take with you that you think will shed some light on a future riddle.

THE ATTIC

"ACHOO! It's very dark and dusty in here!" said Anna, straining to see through the shadows.

If you have not collected a lamp to light your way, go to page 12 .

"The lamplight makes everything look so eerie. Just look at the creepy shadows," said Robert, squinting into the darkness.

"As you would expect, not many people come up here," said Graves, "and so one must assume that this is an ideal place to hide a key clue that could unlock the mystery of the hidden treasure."

"But there is so much here, where should we start?" asked Anna.

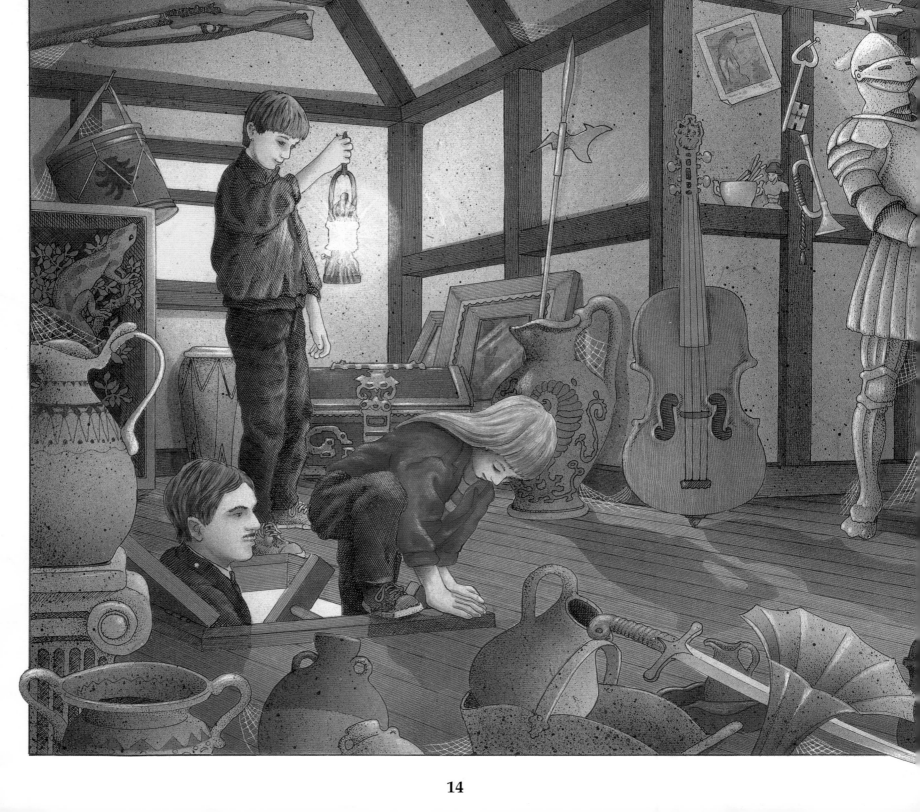

Look closely at all the objects and select one to take with you that you think will be of use later. Of all the objects stored in the attic, only two are identical. Find them both. Take a closer look at the shadows. They are all cast by visible objects with the exception of one. Which shadow has no object to cast it? When you have completed the tasks, turn to page 18.

THE KITCHEN

"Ah, good! Just what I need – more kitchen hands!" bellowed the chef through the mist and hustle and bustle of the hot kitchen. "Oh, yes! It's a busy day and there are mouths to feed and pots to watch. There are things just piling up to be scrubbed, peeled, sliced, and blanched. Just step right up and lend a hand."

"Actually, we aren't kitchen hands, we're..." began Robert.

"That's enough chatter, there is work to be done and you can never have too many cooks to spoil the soup!" hollered the chef, in a booming voice that echoed off the pans.

"Find me the ingredients to make the Master's favorite dish! I need: a dash of rainbow's end, pink bananas, and square oranges not the common round variety! Fetch me multi-colored spangly moonbeams and blue candy floss, prickly pears, and don't stint on the purple apples! And when you have done, I don't want you cluttering up the place. Graves, the butler, will take you on your way before you fall into a vat of boiling oil and end up as dish of the day."

When you have found all the ingredients, take a good, hard look around the kitchen to find the two utensils that are identical. Make a fast exit from the kitchen by turning to page 10 or page 12.

THE MUSEUM

"Boy!" exclaimed Robert. "No wonder Mister Strange needs such a large house. I can't believe that anybody can hoard so much junk!"

"Ahem. All of these objects are treasured possessions gleaned from far-flung corners of the globe", said Graves, frostily.

"Well, the mummies decided it was time to go home!" said Anna, staring at the empty sarcophagi.

"Ah, the afternoons drag so when you are undead and I'm afraid they often wander," said Graves, ruefully. "Sadly, Ramses' sense of direction is not all it once was and he is prone to getting lost."

Unravel the bandage trails to see which route each of the mummies has taken. If you wish to follow Ramses, turn to page 20. If you favor Farouk, go to page 22.

Before you leave the museum, there are two hidden identical objects for you to find that will give you a further clue to the location of the treasure. There is also a compass, which you should collect to help Ramses find his way home.

RAMSES

FAROUK

THE GARDENS

"Ah! Here are the other guests. Mister Strange loves costume parties and this one seems to be in full swing," said Graves, cheerfully.

"Oh, look!" exclaimed Anna. "Is that Ramses wandering in the maze?"

"Most probably," said Graves, tiredly. "It will be some time before he finds his way out! But turn your attention to the party guests. You will notice that the guests have come in pairs with matching outfits."

"Oh, yes!" exclaimed Robert. "I can see two clowns and two boy scouts!"

Match the other pairs of guests to find the odd one out whose partner is hidden in the maze flying a kite. When you have matched all the pairs, follow the maze to help poor Ramses find his way home. Then go to page 22 to continue your quest.

THE CELLAR

"Look, it's Farouk! Why is he in such a hurry?" asked Robert.

"Sadly the ancient king suffers from arachnaphobia!" explained Graves.

"Do you mean he is afraid of spiders?" asked Anna, with a giggle.

"Precisely!" said Graves "But on to more important matters. There is treasure to be found and this seems to be as good a place as any to look for it."

Before you begin to look, you will need a key. If you haven't picked up a key on your journey, go to page 14 and continue the quest.
If you have the key, take a closer look at the chests. Each chest has a padlock and a coat of arms symbol. Find the chest that has a padlock that matches the key and has Mister Strange's coat of arms.

An observant treasure hunter will have noticed the same coat of arms appearing in previous rooms time and time again. If you cannot recognize the correct coat of arms, return to page 8 and open your eyes. You may then return to this page immediately. When you have found the correct chest, collect your booty on page 24, but not until you have collected 13 spiders to put Farouk out of his misery.

CONGRATULATIONS!

You have unlocked the secret of the hidden treasure and have proved to be an ace treasure hunter! But how observant were you along the way? If you didn't notice Mister Strange watching your every move, then take another look in each of the rooms to see if you can spot him! As an extra clue, he is sometimes disguised as a knight bearing his family coat of arms.

SOLUTIONS

THE MAIN ENTRANCE
There are five people watching you: one either side of the left gate-post, one by the right gatepost, one to the right of Anna and one on the far right above the railings.

THE STUDY
To complete the jigsaw puzzle, you need the piece on the floor by the chair at the bottom of page 12 and the large piece on the lefthand side of the table on page 13. Collect the lamp on Anna's right before going to the attic.

THE MUSEUM
The two identical objects are wine cases – one on the lower shelf behind the dinosaur skeleton, the other below the mammoth. The compass is in the statue's hand at the bottom righthand corner of page 19.

THE MAIN HALL
The missing painting is in the box below the suit of armor and Anna on page 8. The replica is in the box to the right and the original is directly above at the top of page 8. Mister Strange's coat of arms appears on the suit of armor and the stained glass window has the treasure chest key as its design.

THE ATTIC
Pick up the key hanging to the left of the central suit of armor. There are two identical drums: one to the left of Robert on page 14 and one at the top of page 15 above the clock. The shadow with nothing to cast it is to the right of the rocking horse shadow and this is cast by Mister Strange.

THE GARDEN
The party guests are paired as follows:
1 & 38   2 & 34   3 & 35   4 & 10   5 & 25   7 & 29
8 & 17   9 & 27   10 & 4   11 & 21   12 & 39   13 & 28
14 & 20   15 & 26   16 & 24   17 & 8   18 & 33   19 & 30
20 & 14   21 & 11   22 & 31   23 & 32   24 & 16   25 & 5
26 & 15   27 & 9   28 & 13   29 & 7   30 & 19   31 & 22
32 & 23   33 & 18   34 & 2   35 & 3   36 & 43   38 & 1
39 & 12   40 & 41   41 & 40   43 & 36.
Number 37 is Mister Strange, 42 is Graves and so the Yeoman Guard (number 6) is the partner of the guest in the maze.

THE TROPHY PASSAGE
The safe path to follow is the row of triangular-patterned tiles and there are fourteen hidden creatures watching you, plus Mister Strange.

THE KITCHEN
The ingredients are found as follows: rainbow's end – directly above Robert; pink bananas – to the left of Robert; square oranges – to the right of Anna; multi-colored, spangly moonbeams – on the left of the kitchen table; blue candy floss – third from the left on the shelf above the children's heads; prickly pears – to the right of Anna; purple apples – on top of the oven next to the range. The two identical objects are corkscrews – one at the left end of the hanging utensil rack, the other in front of the table below the chef's right arm.

THE CELLAR
The correct treasure chest is directly in front of Farouk's face. The 13 spiders appear as follows: four in front of Anna, one behind her, one on the bottom step, two next to the barrel at the bottom of page 23, one on top of the barrel, one on the chest next to the barrel, two on the chest above, one to the left of Robert's foot.

24